QUIT RENTING

A Comprehensive A-Z Guide for First-Time Home Buyers

STEVE UMANSKY

Description

Steve Umansky immigrated to the United States in 2002 with nothing to his name. Today he is a proud homeowner and landlord in the Philadelphia area of Pennsylvania inspiring others to take the same leap going from renter, to homeowner, to landlord, and beyond.

Real estate stands as one of the most powerful and fundamental wealth-building instruments available to everyone, yet it remains significantly underutilized. This book is written as a guide, based on a series of discoveries made along the journey to attaining sustainable financial stability through Real Estate. Successful homeownership can be easy if you plan it out right. I will show you the ropes of purchasing your first home like an expert, and leave you feeling empowered to take control of your own future.

Comparing the choice between homeownership and renting clarifies the best informed decision to make. When you own your home, you're essentially investing in yourself, whereas renting means you're covering someone else's mortgage. In essence, homeownership puts money back in your pocket each month, while renting feels like a monthly contribution to someone else's financial well-being, in addition to the property's appreciating value which is a gain you won't partake in as a renter.

As a property owner, you not only reap the rewards of property appreciation but also build up valuable ownership equity. After all, we all require a place to live, so why not seize the opportunity to own a piece of the American dream? The benefits of homeownership are plentiful, leaving little room for comparison when considering the many major downsides of renting. The material in this book will show you the bigger picture of property ownership. That way you can draw your own conclusion and make the decisions you know to be best.

CONTENTS

WHY BUY A HOME

Why should you choose homeownership over renting, you might wonder? Let's discuss the advantages of owning a home, especially when faced with the prospect of retirement. Imagine you're about to retire at the age of 67, a well-deserved milestone in your life. You've spent years carefully planning your retirement, envisioning a future of comfort and financial security. However, as you take stock of your situation, you notice a concerning trend! Inflation has steadily eroded the purchasing power of your money over the years and is still eating your savings away.

In this moment, reality hits you hard: if you continue to rent, your monthly rental expenses will soon surpass your Social Security income. What does this mean for your financial future? It means that the majority of your income will go towards housing, leaving you with little to enjoy your retirement years and the fruits of your labor that you've worked so hard to earn. All you own are the personal belongings in your rented apartment, and the prospect of relying on a fixed income to make ends meet becomes a daunting reality.

Now, let's consider an alternative scenario. Picture yourself at the same age of 67, but this time, you are the proud owner of a home that has been completely paid off. Your monthly expenses are minimal, mainly consisting of yearly taxes, insurance, and routine maintenance. You have achieved a level of financial freedom that allows you to live comfortably on your own terms.

What's more, you've made strategic investments by acquiring two multifamily rental properties over the years. Through prudent financial management, you've successfully paid off the mortgages on these properties.

As a result, these two rentals continue to generate four rental checks for you every month, effectively putting money in your pocket. These additional rental income streams supplement your Social Security income, ensuring you have the financial means to enjoy your retirement to the fullest. The rental income will be as if you're working a full-time job, but the work is done by your real estate investments. The real question is why would you continue to pay rent when you can build your wealth and own a piece of the American dream?

CHAPTER 1
ASSESS YOUR READINESS

Assessing your readiness is the first and most crucial step to take when you've decided you want to purchase a home of your very own. One of the best benefits to owning a home is the guarantee of a stable monthly payment which builds your ownership equity (your percentage of the ownership in the property) with each payment you make.

To avoid taking on a loan you can't afford or might struggle to pay, before making any financial decision, make sure you've consulted a trusted Mortgage Loan professional to go over all the financials and numbers with you. You want to know beforehand that you can comfortably support your payment while living your desired lifestyle free from any compromise.

Speaking with a professional will allow you to determine what payment to expect depending on the property you wish to acquire, you can then compare the expected payment to your existing housing expenses to use it as a metric and judge what loan amount to take out, that way you can continue making your monthly housing payment realistic to keep up with! On the same note, banks will not approve loans that are beyond a homebuyer's means, with that being said you don't necessarily want to take out the maximum lending limit offered to you because it will be a substantial portion of your income! Overall it's up to you to decide what monetary contribution you feel good paying towards your home every month and you can start to base your purchase budget off of that.

Regardless of the efforts required to get your finances in order, if you have credit card debt it might need to be paid off. Addressing and eliminating high-interest credit card debt along with outstanding monthly payments and delinquencies on your record will go a long way. This will have a huge positive impact on your financial profile and credit score. Unless your mortgage professional can confirm that existing debt won't get in the way of your transaction, your debts will need to be paid. It's a critical step that can't be overlooked. Paying interest rates ranging from 20% to 35% on credit card balances can substantially deplete your savings, funds that could otherwise be better off channeled into real estate investments to grow your wealth.

Additionally, credit cards will hinder your chances of qualifying for loans or credit opportunities because they signify a monthly payment obligation on your personal credit history. This recorded monthly payment will majorly affect income calculations when your financial application is processed and assessed by institutions.

Be sure to pay off all your credit cards and consult your mortgage loan professional about all other debts ahead of time to be sure they won't interfere with your loan approval.

Your mortgage professional's role will be to guide you through all of the loan options available to you and provide you with information on any down payment assistance programs they are aware of. You can also find assistance programs by exploring county websites in the localities and townships you wish to purchase. Such assistance programs can be incorporated into your loan, and save you thousands if not tens of thousands of dollars in closing costs and post-closing reimbursements! Keep in mind not all counties have such programs.

Furthermore, your mortgage professional will primarily consult you on your current financial situation, this includes your personal information such as monthly income, expenses, outstanding debts, delinquencies, and your planned down payment. Once they have an idea of what your finances look like, the next step is to determine what and where you plan to purchase! This includes determining your desired loan amount and researching targeted purchase areas together, to estimate the expected expenses once the property is acquired.

This type of consultation will help you and your mortgage adviser get a better grasp on what possibilities are open to you and your purchase plans. After the mortgage loan professional gets all the required information, they can offer direct advice to a buyer to help accommodate their goals.

If you don't qualify as a buyer and can't get approved for a loan, rest assured a loan officer will help! They will go over your finances to pinpoint what changes are needed from you for you to improve your financial profile. Several reasons can stop you from qualifying as a buyer. These reasons can range from issues such as needing to improve your credit score, to saving more funds, exploring work promotion opportunities, and as discussed earlier paying off outstanding debts or balances. All of which can be improved with time!

Knowing what makes a buyer ready, it's still always worth consulting a loan professional as it's the very first step to assess your readiness in planning a home purchase. If you know your income is solid, your debts are paid, and you have savings, why would you still rent? All you're doing is paying someone else's mortgage for them when you could be paying yours!

CHAPTER 2

THE HOME PURCHASE PROCESS AT A GLANCE

So you've determined you're ready and want to proceed with your big plans to acquire your very first property. You already know you need to speak with your loan officer to professionally assess and help you understand your financial profile through the eyes of a lending institution. Now let's review the full home purchase process at a further glance from the start to the end.

Pre-Approval

Once you have decided what you want to buy, and in which general location you will shop, you must decide what loan size you will take out, and what size of a downpayment you will put down on the home. Based on this information your loan professional will help you officially complete your first step in the purchase process by issuing your personal preapproval letter, granting you eligibility to shop for homes.

Any offer you make on a home will be backed by the bank which did a credit check and an income verification on you. After checking your credit depending on if your score is high or low, it will play a big role in what loan terms you're offered. By issuing the pre-approval letter a bank shows their willingness to finance and fund your purchase. A pre-approval letter will leave sellers no choice but to take your offers very seriously sending you to the list of top buyers above all the other interested groups who approached the seller and were unqualified to make any offer at all.

Offers without a preapproval are rarely accepted however if an unqualified offer is accepted the buyer risks losing all of the deposit money they put down on the home! This can be for any reason that prevents the buyer from closing on the property! The most common reason buyers fail to close on a property and risk their deposit is not qualifying for mortgage financing after the offer has been accepted! Note that a pre-qualification unlike a pre-approval is only an estimate of how much you might be able to borrow based on a brief financial review, not a backed figure supported by completed verifications and a letter.

Home Shopping

Shopping for a home is a process of search, due diligence, and making offers. After you've been preapproved, now comes shopping to find the right home for you! Once your realtor finds and checks out properties within your desired criteria, they will make appointments or come with you to open houses to tour them.

When you've found something you love that you know you want, your realtor needs to do some research on the property's history, neighborhood, and local market conditions. If everything checks out they will consult with you about making an offer, and help aid you in figuring out what kind of offer would make the most sense to put out.

Your offer will often require an earnest money deposit to show you're serious. If your offer is accepted, don't worry the seller can't just take your deposit money and pocket it, it'll be held by the escrow company until it's time to release those funds at closing. Following the acceptance of your offer you'll need the seller or listing agent to provide you or your real estate agent with an agreement of sale.

Home Inspection

Why do Home Inspections matter? Well for any homebuyer first time or not, doing a home inspection is a measure taken to identify hidden problems and plan for repairs. It's an examination of the home's physical condition, from its roof to its foundation. A well-done inspection can prevent costly future surprises.

When it comes to selecting an Inspector choose one with credentials and experience, often best recommended by someone you trust, like your real estate agent or mortgage professional.

Ensure they have a background in the type of home and location you're considering.

When the Inspection Day comes around don't miss it! Attend the inspection to learn about the condition of your potential home to better understand any issues that the inspector may find in its major systems and structural integrity.

Understanding the Inspection Report is essential as it'll detail the inspector's findings. Use it to negotiate repairs from the seller or to determine if you still want to buy the property based on its reported condition. Small issues are not always a deal-breaker as some things can be easily fixed, while others may require a significant amount of work.

With a thorough inspection, you can feel sure in your decision to purchase a particular home you want and like! Overall inspections are ALWAYS worth doing! If a seller is pressuring you into waiving the inspection, note they can likely be hiding something wrong with the home they are selling because a Home Inspection is a very standard step in the process, across all home purchases.

Mortgage Process

The mortgage process, aside from getting your pre-approval letter, begins the moment a property seller accepts your offer and issues you an agreement of sale. You will need to take this agreement of sale also known as a purchase agreement and give the most recent finalized copy of it to your mortgage company for them to add your subject property's information.

Once you've provided the purchase agreement and all other requested loan documents to your trusted loan professional, they will have you sign your initial loan disclosures before taking your mortgage application from the very start and launching it into processing, which will officially put things into motion! Various actions such as inspections, appraisals, title search, and other events will likely take place throughout your mortgage process as well!

Once you provide all the required documents requested by your lender and nothing else remains on the list, your loan's status will be "Clear to Close ". The last step now is attending settlement!

Settlement (Closing)

In preparation for closing, often referred to as settlement, you need to take a good look at the final numbers of your loan making sure you're happy with the monthly payments and all other details of your purchase when the preliminary closing disclosure is issued to you for signature 3 days prior to settlement. You'll then be notified regarding the confirmed date and time your settlement is scheduled to take place! You'll attend a closing meeting where you'll sign all final documents, pay closing costs, and receive the keys to your new home. Your first payment will begin in 1 - 2 months from the date when your purchase closes, giving you time to get your belongings moved in and organized before the payment schedule starts!

CHAPTER 3

GETTING APPROVED FOR A LOAN

As discussed in the prior chapter, securing a preapproval (in the form of a letter) verifying your lender agrees to fund your purchase, is the first step in the home-buying process. Your Loan Officer will play a crucial role in this phase, working closely with you to assess your financial qualifications. Depending on the income sources you plan to utilize for loan qualification, your Loan Officer will request a set of documents aimed at verifying both your income and work history.

One primary focus during this stage is to identify any gaps in your employment timeline over the last two years if there are any. If such gaps exist, your Loan Officer will request a brief explanation, ensuring that your overall financial picture is clearly understood by lenders. It's important to note that your lender will need to verify a 24-month employment history. In case you do have any employment gaps you will need to clarify if they stand in the way of your loan qualification or not. Disruptions in work history may be permissible but need to be documented and explained.

Employment gaps must be documented to show how much income the applying borrower missed out on during the year. Although it's not the end of the world if you have a gap in your employment, it still must be documented and verified to calculate your actual yearly earnings after taking time off from work and what they normally would be if you didn't.

Not everyone has employment gaps, but if you do it's something worth discussing with your loan professional to ensure ahead of time there won't be any problems later in your home purchase process. Lenders send out employment verifications so it's most helpful to communicate vital information early on in the application process before your information is submitted for review.

To begin working on your loan application, mortgage professionals require a standard set of documents. These include:

- Government-Issued Identification: This is crucial to confirm your identity and establish your loan application.
- Tax Returns from the Past Two Years: Providing a comprehensive view of your income, your tax returns offer insights into your income trends over time.
- W-2 Forms from the Past Two Years: These forms detail your yearly earnings and are especially important if you are employed and receive them.

- Recent Pay Stubs: If you are currently employed and receive pay stubs, these will be requested to provide up-to-date information on your earnings.

The meticulous collection of these documents is not only a requirement but in addition, serves as the bedrock for building an accurate profile of your financial standing. Your Loan Officer will utilize these documents, paired with your personal information, to effectively initiate and begin navigating your loan application process.

As you provide these documents, it's important you actively participate in being as openly upfront as possible about your financial history during the construction of your loan application. Any misinformation on a consumer's application will be discovered later on in the process and will jeopardize the purchase. It's required to be clear and truthful about your income, savings, etc. to ensure no complications arise during the mortgage approval process, or at settlement, be open and honest to help lay the groundwork for your successful loan application!

Once you've been approved and consulted about what you can afford, the next step to take is to begin your Home Search!

CHAPTER 4

FINDING A HOME

After preparing for a successful loan approval to be expected later in the process, the next and most exciting step of finding your dream home awaits! Your home search will involve partnering with a reliable and skilled Real Estate Agent. This professional will be instrumental in guiding you to find a property that perfectly matches your specific preferences, requirements, and budget, ensuring a smooth and tailored home-buying experience.

To understand your needs and preferences, take a moment to clearly define your priorities. Consider how many bedrooms you want, what location you desire, which amenities you need, and any other features that are non-negotiable or highly desirable to you. This will allow your Real Estate Agent to help narrow down your search and make house-hunting more efficient by focusing strictly on your desired criteria.

Why use a Real Estate Agent? Because collaborating with an agent is the standard approach taken to significantly streamline your home search! It's standard for the home seller to pay both the buyer's and seller's agents. Meaning it won't save you any money to skip working with an agent. Besides real estate professionals often possess valuable insights into local markets, they can provide access to exclusive listings, and offer guidance for negotiating and purchasing actions. Take advantage of your real estate agent's expertise and knowledge all paid for by the property seller! In addition to being a cost-free service for you, your Realtor is legally bound by a fiduciary duty to prioritize your best interests. This commitment makes the relationship with your Realtor not only beneficial but invaluable in your home-buying journey.

As you explore potential homes, be inquisitive and conduct thorough research on each property. Consider the neighborhood, school districts, local stores, essential services, and potential for future property value appreciation. Utilize online resources, attend open houses, and schedule private viewings to gather as much information as possible about any home you consider making an offer on.

Once you've identified a home to make an offer on, you'll work with your real estate agent to submit a formal offer to the seller. These documents will include the proposed purchase price, any contingencies (conditions that must be met for the sale to proceed), and a proposed timeline for the transaction.

Be prepared to negotiate with the seller. They may counter your offer, and you can respond with adjustments until both parties reach a mutually acceptable agreement to proceed with. Negotiations can involve various terms such as the purchase price, seller's assist, closing date, earnest money deposit amount, and the inclusion of certain appliances, items, or fixtures you'd want to inherit as part of the home sale. Given the complexity involved in purchasing a property, it's crucial to have a professional Realtor representing your best interests. Their expertise and guidance are essential in navigating the intricate process of home buying.

As a tip, remember that no promise made by the seller is valid or will hold up unless it's written into the Purchase Agreement and signed by both parties. Never assume the seller will leave any of the valuables you see within the property during your tour, this includes furniture, appliances, and other belongings. Unless it's stated in the contract that items of value will be left behind for the buyer it's safe to say the seller will take everything valuable with them. Be sure to include those important details. It is standard practice to include all items affixed to the real property in a sale, such as light fixtures and certain drapery. However, to ensure complete clarity and agreement between parties, it is advisable to itemize everything you wish to include in the sale on the inclusion list within the agreement of sale. This step helps guarantee mutual understanding and agreement on what is part of the transaction.

In real estate transactions, the inclusion of an earnest money deposit in your contract is a standard and essential practice, demonstrating your serious commitment to purchasing a particular property. Typically, this process begins with an initial deposit, often a modest sum like $1,000, paid when you make your offer to signify your intent and seriousness. Following this, any additional deposits are usually made after the home inspection and the subsequent negotiations. This additional deposit, which may vary in amount, often serves to reaffirm your commitment, especially in light of any agreed-upon terms or adjustments that arise from the inspection process. Held in an escrow account, this earnest money is eventually credited towards your down payment or closing costs upon finalizing the sale. The specifics, including the amounts and timing of these deposits, can vary based on the agreement between buyer and seller and the local real estate practice standards. It is always prudent to consult with your real estate agent for a clear understanding of the norms and expectations in your particular market.

Once you've reached an agreement with the seller, the next common step is to conduct a Home Inspection, which, as emphasized in Chapter 2, is highly recommended. A professional inspector will evaluate the condition of the seller's property, pinpointing any issues or repairs that may be necessary. Based on the inspection findings, you can either negotiate further with the seller or consider looking for another property. If you decide to proceed and reach a mutual agreement with the seller, they may require a pre-negotiated second Earnest Money Deposit on the home to demonstrate your serious intent to purchase. Again the deposit amount can depend on the home's value but is always negotiable! You should be aware that your deposit won't go straight to the seller, it will be held by an escrow company who will hold the funds and release them after closing. Rest assured if you need help with this, your trusted real estate agent can help negotiate the Earnest Money Deposit amount, help you fill out the check correctly, and aid in delivering it to the escrow company when it comes time to do so!

Overall while envisioning your ideal home, it's crucial to stay within your budgetary constraints. Evaluate the long-term financial commitment, factoring in not just the purchase price but also property taxes, insurance, homeowners' association fees, and potential maintenance costs. Targeting a balance between your aspirational vision and financial ability helps ensure a comfortable and happy homeownership experience that is sustainable in the long term.

Finding a home is an exciting step! With the right tools and insights to navigate this part of the process, you can tackle your home search with confidence and clarity. From defining your preferences to engaging with real estate professionals, and conducting diligent research, each step brings you closer to attaining the new life-changing place you'll soon call home.

CHAPTER 5

THE MORTGAGE PROCESS

Owning a home is often considered a cornerstone of the American Dream. Yet, the path to homeownership is rarely clear or straightforward, especially when it comes to understanding the mortgage process. This chapter aims to demystify this crucial aspect of your home purchase, breaking it down into easy-to-follow steps.

Although we will go over every aspect of the mortgage process throughout this chapter, keep in mind that everything starts with your initial application when you provide your personal information to your loan professional and obtain your Mortgage Pre Approval! That same application is later updated with new information, once you secure your purchase agreement and the subject property completes inspection to your satisfaction. That's why it's absolutely crucial to provide correct information to your loan professional from the very start and share any new changes to your personal finances or credit if they occur!

You should also keep in mind that as discussed in Chapter 1 your debts have a major impact on what kind of home you can afford because they are subtracted away from any income that you show. After your Pre Approval is issued, you should know that taking on any new debt can very likely jeopardize your home purchase as the Pre Approval you are given is based on the expenses documented at the time it was issued to you. Although it's better not to do so at all, in the scenario that you plan to buy a new car, open new credit cards, or take out any new loans before your purchase closes and funds, it's important to understand it will definitely impact how much house you can afford, and can even totally call off your purchase as a result of new debt obligations.

To be safe, first consult your loan professional and find out if you can still afford the home you want by confirming the new debt (car loan, credit card, etc.) won't get in the way. Or alternatively, you might need to wait until your home purchase closes before taking on any additional debt. I certainly cannot restrict you from applying for whichever new loans you wish but be cautious as new unreported consumer credit is one of the most common reasons home purchases don't end up making it to closing. Countless people make this simple and easy mistake which can call an entire purchase off leaving the buyer in a position where they can no longer afford the home they want! This is certainly something to keep in mind when you are getting into the process of buying a home of your very own!

You should generally renew your Pre Approval every 90 days but in some cases much sooner if you know the market interest rates or your personal financial situation has changed. In such an event the numbers previously calculated on your loan application need to be updated to reflect the current market and your personal finances. Be sure your offers on homes are legitimate and will be financed when it comes time to fund your pursuit! You can do this by avoiding new debt and communicating changes to your loan professional so they can see the full picture of your finances and update any old information.

In addition, to avoid new debt, every buyer needs to know NOT to switch jobs during the loan process! Since your work history is crucial in obtaining mortgage financing, any work transitions or current employment changes will impact your loan approval. Again it's best to avoid this altogether, but in the event that this happens to you, be sure to immediately communicate all your employment changes to your loan professional! They will review your situation for further consultation and attempt to resolve the issue!

Moving on from avoiding new debt, and job transitions, and assuming you've prepared and done everything perfectly. Now that the purchase agreement is signed by you and the seller, your mortgage company will need a copy of it! Along with any deposit copies or proof or wires that have been made for the transaction already. After your mortgage company has your purchase agreement and proof of deposit, you'll be provided an initial disclosure package containing approximate closing costs requiring your signature to proceed! Once it's signed, the Title and Appraisal are ordered!

Before discussing the importance of Title and Appraisals, it's important to be aware that the initial Loan Estimate can sometimes vary from the final figures and be higher or lower. This variation is because Loan Officers cannot precisely predict all closing costs from the beginning. Your initial loan estimate is based on the expected figures for real estate taxes and insurance which are estimated, and can be subject to change based on the actual assessments and premiums. The final closing costs are always received 3 days before your closing day via the Closing Disclosures ensuring you have enough time to deal with any potential concerns!

Following initial disclosures, expect to have a standard list of financial documents be requested from you. Upon completing the initial checklist, you'll officially be halfway through the mortgage process!

A clear Title and a satisfactory Appraisal are the goal of every home transaction! Why is that so? What's the importance of your home having a clear Title? While the Deed to a property, is the legal document validating your ownership rights. On the other hand your Title Insurance company assures you that there are no unresolved ownership disputes, liens, or legal issues that could jeopardize your claim of ownership to the property. It's your Title company's job to make sure they find any information that would impede on your property's Title from being considered "clear". In addition, Title insurance is used to protect property owners against unforeseen issues if they ever arise after your purchase! Note that any discovered Title issues will need to be addressed before finalizing your purchase. By appreciating and taking the necessary precautions, you're one step closer to securing your dream home with confidence and peace of mind!

Now that you know about property Title and the importance of it being clear, what's an Appraisal and what purpose does it serve? Appraisals help you and your lender establish the fair market value of the property you're buying. A professional appraiser evaluates the home based on various factors such as its size, condition, location, and comparable sales in the area. The appraisal is crucial because it ensures that you are not overpaying for the property.

Lenders also don't want to over-finance a property more than it is worth! They assess the property's value in relation to the loan amount. If the appraisal comes in below the agreed-upon purchase price, there may need to be a renegotiation with the seller to lower the price, unless you're willing to pay the difference of the subject property's value and sales price out of pocket towards your purchase. Alternatively if your property appraised higher than the sales price then congratulations! You got a great deal on your home!

Finally after you've provided all the documents requested from you, signed all necessary disclosures, your appraisal came back great, and your subject property's Title is Clear.

Your loan will now be submitted for review! At this stage underwriters investigate your loan application looking for any errors, inconsistencies, false information, and making sure verifications have been performed by the mortgage company as needed.

After the underwriting team completes their review of your application and supporting documents, if everything aligns with the submitted information, they will issue a conditional approval for your loan application.

Conditional Loan Approval, allows the delivery of your Loan Commitment Document! This is a critical moment in everyone's home buying journey! This document is essential for realtors because it fulfills one of the contractual contingencies, confirming that the buyer's financing is on track for approval. It's a signal that the loan has undergone a comprehensive review by an underwriter and is conditionally approved!

Again this means that your loan is on track for approval, provided you meet certain specified conditions! These conditions typically include the submission of additional documents requested by the underwriting team. Fulfilling these requirements is essential to push your loan application towards final approval.

There's no use in trying to predict what documents you'll be asked to provide ahead of time, because it varies too much from person to person! But when the final document list is released from underwriting and you've gathered and provided all that's been requested from you to your mortgage company, they will immediately submit your application for final review in anticipation of getting "Clear to Close" loan status, which will indicate your loan is fully approved!

Ensure you schedule a final walkthrough before finalizing your home purchase. This is your opportunity to verify that the property is in the same condition as when initially inspected. The final walkthrough is crucial as it's your last chance to identify and negotiate any unexpected issues with the property before completing the transaction. Paying close attention during this walkthrough can help avoid unforeseen complications later on. It's essential to know what you are buying so look around and inspect everything yourself to be sure it's up to your own standards, this decision is for the long run.

When you've decided you'd like to proceed with your purchase, your mortgage company will help you schedule your closing time. Your closing is most likely to take place at the Title company's office, but can be at any other mutually agreed upon location that is acceptable for hosting settlement and signing paperwork! At closing, be prepared to bring a certified check to cover the closing costs. Your mortgage company will also provide assistance and guidance if you need any help understanding these costs or what you need to bring. Their support will ensure a smooth and well-informed closing process.

CHAPTER 6

WHAT TO EXPECT AT CLOSING

Closing on your chosen home is the last step in your successful home-buying journey. In this chapter, we'll walk you through the process, step by step, to demystify what happens at closing and to prepare you for this pivotal moment. Your closing date is a critical milestone. It's the day you finalize the purchase and officially become the owner of your new home. The closing date is typically agreed upon during the early negotiation.

The most crucial step before closing is reviewing your Closing Disclosure. As mentioned in the prior chapter, this document is received at least three days before closing, serving the purpose of outlining the final mortgage loan details, including the exact closing costs! Before signing any home-binding paperwork you'll be informed of your closing costs and instructed to either bring a certified check or arrange a wire transfer for these costs.

Apart from checking to make sure your closing disclosure has a closing cost and monthly payment you agree with, you'll additionally need to conduct a final walkthrough of the home you're purchasing. The final walkthrough of the property will be your last chance to check that everything is in order, and functions to your satisfaction! This step is vital to ensure there are no last-minute issues with the property.

When it comes to signing the final documents to get your keys, prepare for a significant amount of paperwork! The most important documents you'll encounter include the mortgage note, which is your promise to repay the loan. The mortgage or deed of trust, which is what secures the mortgage note, and the closing disclosure, summarizing the details of your mortgage. All of the mentioned paperwork will require your review and signature to conclude the transaction.

Moving on to the most rewarding part of closing! Receiving the keys to your new home! Once all the paperwork is signed and the seller receives the funds, the property is officially yours. After your closing, you may need to take care of a few administrative tasks, such as filing school applications for your children with the school district, transitioning the utilities to your name, and of course planning your move! Now that you have acquired your home you can stop paying rent and work towards building your future instead of your landlords! Enjoy the comfort of owning and taking care of what is truly yours while pitching into your finances and retirement!

CHAPTER 7

POTENTIAL ROADBLOCKS TO HOMEOWNERSHIP

Poor Credit:

Having a poor credit score is the easiest way to get declined for a mortgage loan. A poor credit score can be the result of a few things, the most major one being missed debt payments. Be sure to stay on top of your bills by paying them on time! Each missed payment will contribute to lowering your credit score! If your credit cards aren't paid, make your best effort to pay them off while keeping the credit lines open (don't close the cards or it'll hurt your score).

Switching jobs During the Loan Process:

Because Mortgage Lenders are required to verify your employment over a 24 month history, unfortunately switching jobs after you've received your Pre Approval letter or anytime later in the process will at least disrupt, if not completely ruin your ability to purchase a home. Consult your Loan Professional and discuss your work transition to see how it will impact your purchase plans!

Rushing to find a house

Rushing to find a house can lead to many mistakes. This can include placing too high of an offer on a property! Not knowing what options and amenities are available to you at your price point! Or worst of all ending up with a property you don't like that you wish you could trade for another. Instead of falling into this trap consult your Real Estate Agent and talk through your plans, take the necessary time to explore your options, and know what you're placing an offer on! Only make a move after you've considerately found and picked a house you truly love, that you know you'll enjoy long term.

> **TIP**: You should only rush to place an offer on super desirable homes, properties selling at discount (below market value), or deals your Real Estate Agent recommends moving on quickly in which case you'll want to be first to contact the seller.

Neglecting Home Inspection

There can be many things said regarding the condition of the property you're buying, but overall you must be satisfied with it as the property you're buying will be yours! Therefore It's your job to walk the premises to see its up to your standards, and the inspectors job to find hidden faults that are not easily seen by you. DO NOT ignore anything displeasing to you, address your property concerns from the time of the inspection up until the final walkthrough before your settlement!

Skipping the Pre-Approval Process

Unless you are prepared to purchase a property for its full cash asking price, and you have the money sitting in your bank account, you'll need a Mortgage Pre approval letter validating that a Lender will finance your plans. You should not be making any offers on homes without consulting a Loan Professional, because it's always the first step to every home purchase! Even your Realtor won't be able to show you homes until you are Pre Approved, and will also direct you to see a Loan professional before home shopping. Sellers won't take you or your offer seriously, unless you show them a Pre Approval letter. However even in the event that your offer gets accepted you will most often need to put up a substantial earnest money deposit, which you risk totally losing for misrepresenting that you could buy the home if you fail to close on the property. With changing markets you never know what you do or don't qualify for today, so it's better not to guess and be sure by trusting a pro with the math behind that! Needless to say, avoid this common trap!

Not Having funds for Closing

This potential pitfall is self explanatory yet important to avoid. Lacking the funds for settlement will at least delay closing if not cancel it completely. Avoid going through the entire home purchase process with no result! Confirm your closing costs ahead of time, by getting a rough estimate as early as during your Pre Qualification or Pre Approval phase!

Providing False or Fraudulent Information

Providing false or fraudulent information in an attempt to obtain a Loan is not only punishable by law, but ineffective at its goal. The Mortgage Loan Process largely consists of thorough verifications and checks aimed at pinpointing inaccuracies and misinformation. Any false personal information such as names, addresses, social security numbers, Etc. will be discovered at some point in the process. Same goes for income information and work history! Hidden information, which is crucial for your lender to know, is always discovered due to the high level resources available to lenders. There's no use in hiding information which will be discovered later, instead be upfront with your lender so they can talk you through all of your available options and steps to take so you can be well prepared when it comes time to take action!

Failing to plan for the Future:

When buying a home, you should already know it isn't a small decision! That's why when you're Pre Approved and shopping for one, you need to think about your future. Ask yourself questions like: Do I want to live here for 1 year or 5 years? Do I need to remodel anything? Will my family grow in size? Can the storage space available hold my expanding collection of belongings? Is the location of the home I like a practical distance from my work? Is this close enough to visit my relatives? Is there space to invite my friends over on the weekend? There are countless questions to ask yourself before making your mind up and committing to a choice! Think about your future and Plan!

THE HIDDEN COSTS OF RENTING

In conclusion, the decision to rent a home may seem like a convenient and straightforward choice, but the true cost goes beyond the monthly rent payment. In the bigger picture, making the choice to rent your home can potentially be the quickest and easiest way to rob yourself of a secure retirement. While everyone's need for a place to live is undeniable, the quality of life is significantly higher for homeowners than it is for renters.

The financial implications of renting are substantial and often underestimated. When you rent, you're essentially contributing to someone else's investment, building their equity instead of your own. It's a continuous cycle of payments that doesn't offer any return on investment for the renter. In contrast, homeownership provides a unique opportunity to build equity and secure financial stability.

Owning a home is a tangible investment that holds value over time. As property values generally appreciate, homeowners experience an increase in their net worth. This increase is a result of both the property's appreciation and the gradual reduction of the mortgage balance through regular payments. Essentially, when you own a home, you're not just paying for housing, you're investing in your future of financial security.

The journey to homeownership might seem daunting initially. The process involves navigating through various financial intricacies, understanding mortgage options, and finding the right property. It can be frustrating, but the benefits far outweigh the challenges. With the guidance of a trusted loan professional, the path to homeownership becomes clearer.

Your loan professional is a crucial ally in this journey. They possess the knowledge and expertise to guide you through the intricate process of securing a mortgage. From understanding your financial situation to helping you choose the right mortgage product, they play a vital role in ensuring that you are well-prepared for the responsibilities of homeownership.

While the initial steps into homeownership might be challenging, the long-term rewards are worth the effort. Building equity in a property is like investing in your own financial security. It's a tangible asset that can appreciate over time and provide stability.

Overall, renting may seem like the easy way out, but it comes at a significant cost – a cost that extends far beyond the monthly rent payment. Choosing to own your home is an investment in your future, a step towards financial stability, and a move that empowers you to shape your own destiny. So, while the journey to homeownership might be challenging, it's a journey well worth taking. The interest rate on rent is 100% of your payment!

BONUS: HOUSE HACKING METHOD

This bonus section will outline house hacking and the ideal sequence to execute it perfectly! It's precisely the strategy I employed when acquiring my first home, and it's the same blueprint I recommend for your home purchase journey. In a nutshell, "House Hacking" is when you live in part of your property while renting out the rest! It's an increasingly popular strategy for building wealth through real estate.

Emphasizing that each property (in your future portfolio) can be purchased with a minimal down payment of 5%, you'll take advantage of this underutilized approach by buying each property as your primary residence, and residing there for at least one year before renting it out. This strategy will allow you to build a million dollar rental portfolio with minimal investment, using bank financing as leverage! My suggestion is to regard your initial property purchase as a stepping stone toward your millionaire real estate portfolio. This simply means purchasing your first property with a forward-thinking vision to transform it into a rental investment at a later stage.

Ideally, your first property should be a multifamily dwelling—a duplex, triplex, or quadplex—where you can reside in one of the units while leasing the others to offset your monthly property expenses and simultaneously amass ownership in your investment. By purchasing a multifamily property as your first residence you maximize your future cash flow.

This type of property is ideal for individuals or couples who are comfortable starting out with a smaller space and with neighbors in the same building. Despite a smaller living space, you will maximize your property's income potential by renting out all additional housing units, as well as your unit, if you move out and upgrade to a larger home. If you aspire to have a large single home one day, with your financial future in mind, I urge you to wait and make a few investments first!

House Hacking Purchase Sequence

STEP 1: Multi Family Home

The best possible way to begin your purchase journey is with a multifamily home, such as a duplex or triplex. These properties are excellent for generating rental income while living on-site. The 5% down payment as a primary residence makes this a financially accessible option.

STEP 2: Condo

A condo is an excellent next step, particularly in urban areas. The reduced maintenance responsibility, often covered by homeowners' association fees, makes it a convenient choice. With a 5% down payment, it's an affordable entry into homeownership.

STEP 3: Townhome

A townhome strikes a balance between a condo and a single-family home. It offers more space and, typically, lower maintenance responsibilities. This property type is attractive for small families and professionals.

STEP 4: Twin Home

A twin home offers a semblance of detached living while still being manageable in size. It's a viable option in your house hacking journey.

STEP 5: Small Single Home

A small single-family home involves taking on significant property management. It's still relatively easy to maintain and can attract long-term tenants, making it a steady and solid investment.

STEP 6: Large Home or Forever Family Home

Finally, consider investing in a large home or what you envision as your forever family home. While this requires more maintenance and cost, it offers a long-term residence for your family. You can consider this home a well earned reward for diligently investing in your future and creating your rental empire.

House Hacking Summary

This sequential approach to purchasing property known as House Hacking allows you to gradually scale up your real estate investments. Starting from a multifamily home to eventually acquiring your forever family home! The advantage of this strategy is using the minimal down payment requirement when purchasing each property as your primary residence. This approach not only fosters financial growth, but also provides a practical experience in property management. By following this structured path, you can effectively navigate the world of real estate investing, starting with a modest initial contribution that will snowball overtime, and turn into an expanding real estate investment portfolio.

MOST COMMON MYTHS ABOUT BUYING A HOME

Myth: Renting is Always Cheaper than Buying

Reality: While renting may have lower upfront costs, buying a home can be more cost-effective over the long term, as you build equity and potentially benefit from tax deductions.

Myth: You Need a Large Down Payment to Buy a Home

Reality: Many mortgage programs offer options with low down payments, such as FHA loans, VA loans, and conventional loans with as little as 3% down. Down payment assistance programs are also available in some areas.

Myth: Your Credit Has to Be Perfect to Get a Mortgage

Reality: While a better credit score can help secure a more favorable interest rate, there are mortgage programs available for borrowers with less-than-perfect credit.

Myth: You Should Buy as Much House as You Can Afford

Reality: It's crucial to stay within your budget and not overextend yourself. Consider your long-term financial goals and the associated costs of homeownership, including property taxes, insurance, and maintenance.

Myth: You Can't Buy a Home with Student Loan Debt

Reality: Having student loan debt doesn't automatically disqualify you from getting a mortgage. Lenders consider your debt-to-income ratio and other financial factors when assessing your eligibility.

Myth: You Can Buy Any Home With a Mortgage

Reality: A home must be considered in livable and functional condition before a mortgage bank will finance a loan on it. In addition, some banks will hesitate and refuse to finance properties located in "disaster areas" which typically have a prior history that could still impact the home going into the future.

Myth: Your Mortgage Payment is the Only Housing Cost

Reality: Homeownership comes with ongoing expenses, including property taxes, homeowners' insurance, maintenance, and potentially homeowners' association (HOA) fees. It's essential to budget for all these costs.

Myth: You can Shop for Homes Without Consulting a Mortgage Professional

Reality: Unless you're prepared to buy a property for its full purchase price and have the full cash amount in your bank, making offers on a home and signing a contract is a terrible idea. Without looking into your personal finances to guarantee you'll qualify for your desired loan amount you'll surely lose any deposit you gave the seller for a false representation of your ability to buy what you've made an offer on.

Myth: Spending Money on Home Improvement is Wasting Money

Reality: Depending on the renovations you complete not only will you benefit from enjoying them but you'll increase your home value in the event that you ever decide to sell it

Myth: Skipping the Final Walkthrough for My Purchase is Okay because I've already seen the Property and know what it looks like

Reality: Don't Ever Skip the Final Walkthrough before closing, be sure to conduct a thorough final walkthrough to see the property is in the agreed-upon condition and that any negotiated repairs have been made.

Myth: Banks can raise your Mortgage Payment Anytime

Reality: All fixed-interest mortgages have the same monthly payment which will never increase on the borrower for the life of the loan. The payments that most frequently fluctuate up or down are your property taxes and insurance which the bank does not decide or set. These payments are not the same as the principal and interest payments made to the bank.

Personal Key Takeaways

(continued)

(continued)

51

(continued)

(continued)

(continued)

(continued)

(continued)

(continued)

(continued)

(continued)

(continued)

(continued)

61